9781845333843

D1785239

Lilies

OLIVER E. P. WYATT

Chairman, R.H.S. Lily Committee

LONDON

The Royal Horticultural Society

1972

Contents

Photographs by R. J. Corbin
Line drawings by Jill Cox

Lilies

This is a booklet about lilies for all those gardeners who have not seriously tried to grow these wonderful plants. It suffers from the limitations inseparable from a book of this kind that it is neither as accurate nor as comprehensive as it should be since it aims at being concise.

It deals with the true lilies, that is plants given the botanical name of *Lilium* and not all those other plants (lovely as they may be), also called "lilies"; water lily, lily of the valley, day lily, Kaffir lily, Scarborough lily, Guernsey lily, canna lily, arum lily and many others, nor does it attempt to deal with growing lilies in pots.

Only those true lilies which are easy to grow and hardy will be suggested to the reader. There are some species which are grown in only a few gardens and cannot be bought from nurserymen, and these will receive little or no attention in the following pages.

My aim is to encourage you to grow lilies. Whatever your soil and conditions, you are bound to succeed with some of them; but as you progress in your enthusiasm—as you surely will—you must expect to have your setbacks and disappointments. But what are these but incentives to try again?

Don't say you cannot afford lilies; don't tell me that lilies will not grow in the limey soil which you have; don't tell me that you have no heated greenhouse—I will accept none of these excuses! But the advice given in this pamphlet is perhaps a counsel of perfection; and if you follow thirty per cent of it, you will probably grow lilies quite well.

1. Geographical distribution and characters

No lilies have been found growing wild in the southern hemisphere. But in the temperate zone of the northern hemisphere they range from Japan, Manchuria, China, Siberia, the Himalaya, Asia Minor to Europe, and the west and east coasts of North America. As you learn more about lilies you will find that the locality in which they are found is of some importance in relation to their cultivation, e.g. those which are native of Japan or the eastern side of America need an acid soil and those which grow wild in Europe or China mostly prefer or tolerate a limey soil.

It would be simple if all the lilies with trumpet-shaped flowers came from one region, all those with turk's cap flowers from another and all chalice-shaped flowers from another; but this is not so, and flowers of almost every shape are found in most of the zones.

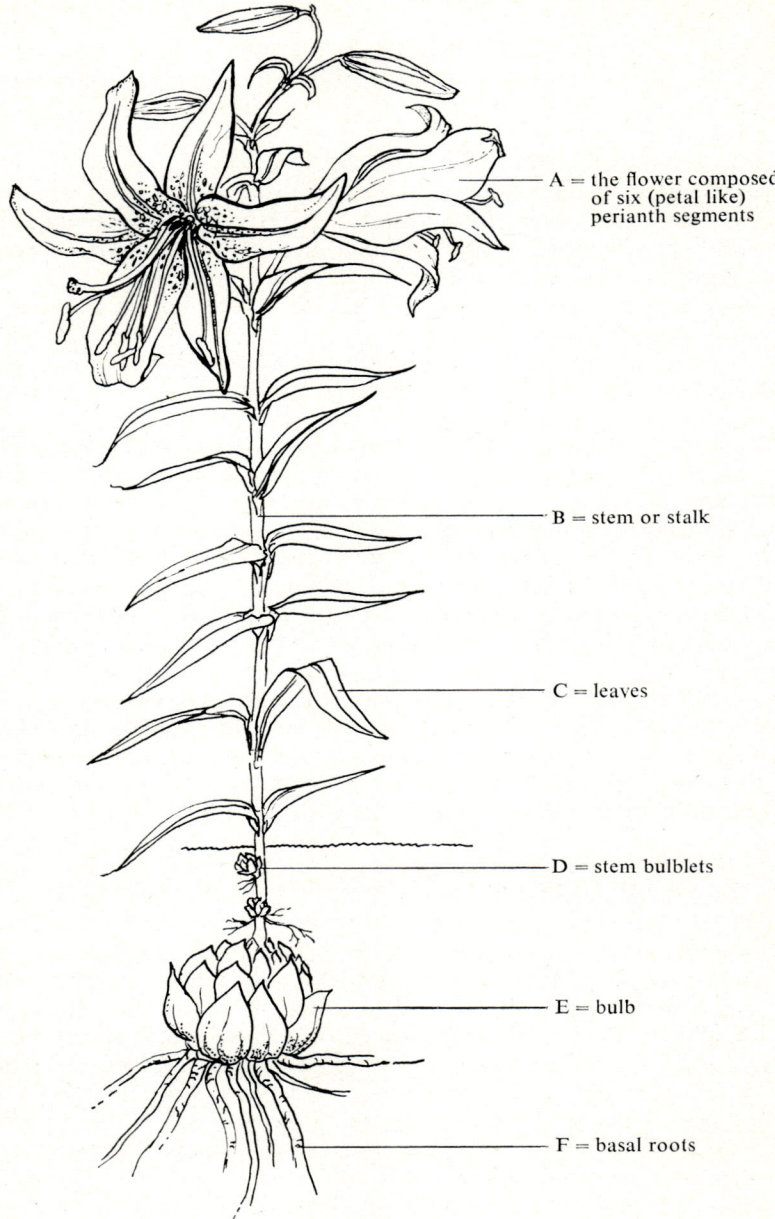

A = the flower composed of six (petal like) perianth segments

B = stem or stalk

C = leaves

D = stem bulblets

E = bulb

F = basal roots

Fig. 1. Diagram of a lily plant

4

Flower colours are mostly white, yellow, orange or red, or some combination of these. But anyone who visited the Oregon breeding farms and saw lilies in flower there would be amazed by the range of colour which has been evolved. There seem to be flowers of every colour except blue.

The first consideration in the choice of lilies to grow must be the nature of the soil in your garden. Some lilies will not grow in lime; a few prefer it; and most will tolerate it. But fortunately many of the easiest lilies will make a brave show in any garden provided that a little trouble is taken in preparation of the soil and in cultivation.

Some ardent lily growers prefer to grow only the species (i.e. lilies as found in the wild); they claim that they have a grace and charm which is lost in many of the "man-made" lilies. But I would say that many of the hybrids (raised by crossing the species) have great beauty and are most desirable and easy garden plants.

Almost all hybrids between species were produced by crossing lilies from the same geographical area, so that a first generation hybrid between two Japanese lilies will almost certainly require an acid soil, whereas one between two Chinese species (for instance) will be tolerant of lime. But now generations of hybrids from all parts of the world have been crossed with one another, and so far as their soil requirements are concerned one has to depend on knowledge of the types, or on information given in the nurserymen's catalogues, or on experiment.

2. Sites in the garden, and soils

The ideal site for lilies is a woodland glade. But few of us have this in the garden, so we have to try and make comparable conditions. Lilies like to have their heads in the sun and their feet in the shade. This presents little difficulty in most gardens: they can be planted among low-growing shrubs and azaleas where they conveniently provide colour after the shrubs have flowered, or else amongst annuals. They can be planted among herbaceous plants, but some of these, such as paeonies, are greedy feeders and are apt to devour more than their share of the food provided for the lilies.

The great essential for growing lilies well is good drainage. Whatever your soil type, you must provide this. There are some lilies which are described as "swamp lilies" and people have been deceived by their name into thinking that they will grow in a marsh. It is true that in the wild they grow in damp places, but they are in fact found on hummocks so that the bulb is never water-logged though the roots can get down to running water.

And the second essential is that the soil should always be kept moist. An extra help in keeping up the content of soil moisture is to dig in before planting a good mixture of peat and leaf-mould which absorbs and retains the moisture.

The soil need not be rich; in the wild some lilies grow in very poor soil, but growth tends to be stunted if there is insufficient nourishment for the bulb. Most soils need only a little extra preparation before planting. If you have a light soil all that is necessary is to dig into it a quantity of peat or well-decayed leaf-mould to a depth of about 18 inches (it is surprising to what depths lily roots will descend). If it is a soil only a few inches deep over chalk or stone this must be dug out to a depth of 18 inches and replaced with soil that has been mixed with leaf-mould, peat and sand. Leaf-mould which is insufficiently rotted down is liable to become mildewy. The best kind of peat is sedge or bush bog peat; peat dug up from moorlands tends to be too acid. The best sand for use with lilies is coarse silver sand.

If your soil is heavy clay, some hard work is needed. I had an area 20 yards by 10 yards, where I wanted to grow lilies. I cut down the laurels on it, started to dig it over and found that a few inches down was a two-foot layer of heavy sticky clay; below that was a more sandy clay which seemed permeable. I was determined to grow lilies there; so I dug six holes each four foot in diameter, and dug down right through the clay; filled the holes some way with stones and rubble (one with faggots of wood, which was equally successful) and then filled the top 18 inches with suitably mixed soil. The drainage was perfect below the lilies and the moisture seeped in from the surrounding clay and kept the roots damp. Never did lilies grow better.

But this may be too strenuous an exercise for most gardeners. If you cannot dig through the clay, you will probably be wise to grow the lilies in a raised bed. Dig out the soil to a depth of a foot or so and fill in to almost ground level with stones or rubble. Then build up a bed to a foot or so high consisting of some of the better of your soil mixed with leaf-mould, peat and sand (or you can buy in top soil). You can build up the sides of the bed with stones or logs, or if you feel extravagant, with railway sleepers, or you can allow the sides to slope away very gently. But if you have clay you must at all costs work it well before thinking of planting; dig in decaying leaves and as much coarse sand as you can afford in the previous winter; decaying leaves seem to have the effect of breaking up the clay. Fork the soil over in the winter, exposing it to frost and sun and rain and then in the spring dig in your leaf-mould or peat. Lilies dislike farmyard manure unless it is well decayed and two or three years old; so don't use fresh manure.

3. Planting

Your lily bed or site has been prepared for some time and the soil has sunk, your bulbs have arrived and you are ready to plant them. Fork in a little general fertilizer* or bone meal or wood ash, at about two handfuls per square yard. You hope that the roots of the lilies are still fresh and have not shrivelled. Lily roots are never wholly dormant (as are those of a daffodil or tulip), and though it is difficult for a nurseryman to keep the bulbs fresh they should always be firm and the roots should not be broken off. You hope too that they are young bulbs, for when young bulbs are planted they grow "contractile" roots (opaque and soft and growing straight down from the bulb) which pull the bulb down to whatever level in the soil suits it best; once these roots are broken off or decay, the bulb does not travel any more and just has to do its best at the level at which you have planted it.

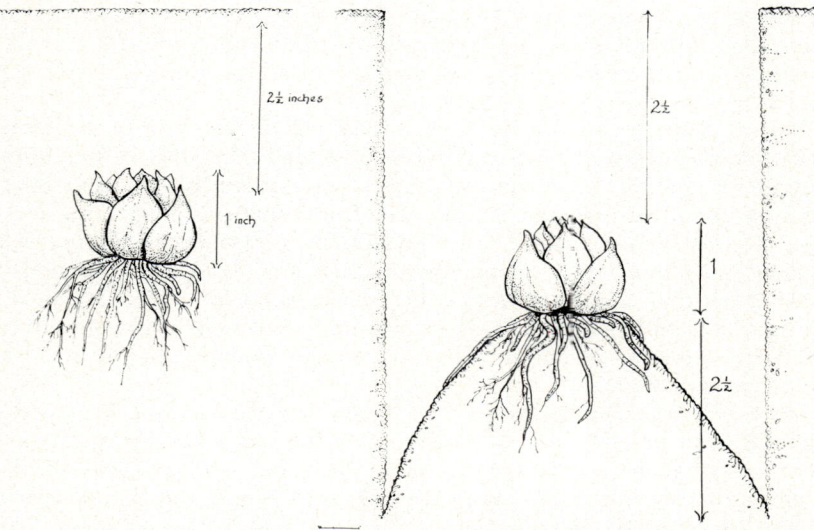

Fig. 2. Normal planting depth, left; planting on a 'volcano', right

The correct depth depends on the type of soil; the lighter the soil, the deeper the bulb should be, perhaps two inches deeper in a light soil than in clay. As a general rule the shoulder of the bulb should be below the surface $2\frac{1}{2}$ times the height of the bulb. But the bulbs of the Madonna lily (*L. candidum*) and of *Cardiocrinum* should be planted with the nose just above the surface of the ground, and *L.* × *testaceum* only just below.

*A general fertilizer contains approximately equal parts of the three main plant nutrients; nitrogen, potash and phosphate. Several good commercial brands are available on the market.

Suppose your bulb measures about one inch from its shoulder to its base, make a hole for it about 6 inches deep with a trowel, then form a "volcano" at the bottom of the hole (the top of the "volcano" being 1 plus $2\frac{1}{2}$ inches below the surface), put the bulb on top of the volcano and spread out the roots around the slopes. Fill in round the roots, and around the bulb put in plenty of coarse sand. This helps (a) to keep the bulb clean, (b) to deter slugs, (c) to find the bulb (or where it once was) if you want to dig it up. Then fill in level with the surface. Put more sand on top of the bulb as you fill in so that slugs are deterred from burrowing from above. I always mark every bulb I plant with a stick, this makes it easier to weed and to treat.

Distance apart. Spacing clearly depends on the height of the plant. *Cardiocrinum* which grows to 12 feet, should be 5 or 6 feet apart; *Lilium auratum* which grows up to 8 feet, say 4 feet apart; but some of the smaller plants such as *L. pumilum* or *L. duchartrei*, which grow to $2\frac{1}{2}$ to 3 feet, need only 6 or 8 inches between them.

Time to plant. Most gardeners like to plant their lilies before the winter (if they can persuade their nurseryman to send the bulbs early). Many experts nowadays move their own lilies as soon as they have flowered (and cut off about half the stem). It has been found that it is a help to a lily to get its roots partly established in the autumn. *L. candidum* (odd man out again) must be moved by September because it has only a short period of dormancy and starts growing again in late summer—green leaves will appear in October. *Cardiocrinum* species must be planted before the winter. But providing the ground is neither frozen nor sodden, other lilies can be planted until March.

If by chance your bulbs come in frosty weather or have had a long journey from abroad and are in a state of dessication, your best chance is to box or pot them in a mixture of damp peat and sand and give them a chance to fatten up again. Then when growth begins and the weather is right, they can be planted out.

4. After care

Overwintering. Early in the winter I go round my lilies, remove the dead stems, pull them up or if still firm, cut them off at soil level, put a handful of sand on each (marked by a stick—you remember) and then a handful of leaf-mould or peat. This gives just a little protection against frost and foe.

Some people have found that a layer of old pine needles on the soil surface before the winter is helpful. I cannot say that I have found this notably successful; but it is of interest that a large number of lilies in the wild are found in or near coniferous forests.

Feeding. When March comes round I put a handful of general fertilizer on each and just fork it into the sand and leaf-mould. Many lilies grow roots from the stem above the bulb and just below the surface of the ground, as well as from the base of the bulb, so that for them this bit of feeding is rather important. A little general fertilizer should be given throughout the season at monthly intervals until flowering.

Tying and staking. Some lilies do not need support, but most do. I try to avoid using a bamboo cane if I can help it, since frequent tying is needed and when the lilies flower they look stiff and artificial. They may be planted behind some tall shrub which will give support, in which case they can be left to themselves. But generally I stake them with pea sticks. It is difficult to judge the ultimate height, but make the sticks taller than you think you will want, and then it is easy to bend over or break the twigs as need be. This supports the lily well, and if the sticks are put in early enough (about March) the stems grow up through the sticks which are then concealed by the lily leaves. Later in the summer the supports are almost invisible.

You must watch for slugs and catch them with bait, especially in wet weather at the time when the spikes are pushing through the ground. You must watch for the leaves becoming spotted with brown or turning brown (since this may be the start of botrytis disease) and pick off these leaves and burn them. And if leaves become striped with yellow or if flowers become contorted, this may be the start of some virus disease. If you have the courage—and it is most painful to have to do it!—it is wiser to pull up the whole of the infected plant, bulb and all, and burn it lest greenfly carry the disease to other lilies and infect them, for there is no known cure. (Pests and diseases are dealt with more fully on pp. 21–3 of this booklet).

Transplanting. As with planting, transplanting should be carried out from mid-September to late October. Few lilies, if any, require regular transplanting; the majority should be left undisturbed. *L. pardalinum* and its hybrids such as 'Shuksan' are notable exceptions as the bulbs increase rapidly if happy, forming large clumps of interlocked bulbs. Flowering of these clumps gradually becomes less and less until it almost stops. Such clumps should be lifted and the younger, outer bulbs replanted, preferably in a new site or at least in soil which has been thoroughly enriched, as should be done when any lily is transplanted.

If a group of lilies seems to be "going back" or losing its vigour or becoming too crowded, it is sometimes worth while to replant the lilies in a newly prepared site. But it must be remembered that almost all bulbs, of every kind, do tend to deteriorate in old age and depend on renewal by reproduction by one means or other. So an aged group of lilies may have failed to renew themselves and may be beyond recall.

5. Propagation

Seed. I want to use all my powers of persuasion to encourage the amateur to grow his lilies from seed. It is easy, it is cheap, since a packet of seeds can be bought for a few pence, he can obtain a good clump as distinct from a few individual bulbs, and above all he will have a stock free from disease. A later section of this booklet deals with some pests and diseases, but the point here is that the main lily diseases are not normally carried in seeds, whereas many of those bulbs which are bought have disease within them even if it is latent. Nurserymen are not to blame, they take every possible care to see that the bulbs which they send out are in good health. But disease in bulbs is not easy to detect in its early stages and in spite of great care some diseased bulbs do get on the market. It is often said to me that bought bulbs flower well the first year and then deteriorate rapidly. Conditions for growing them may be wrong, but normally it is because the bulbs when received are already infected and begin to die as soon as the disease gets a hold.

The only objection to growing lilies from seed is that seed from hybrid lilies do not breed true; you will not get seedlings exactly like the parent. You may get lilies somewhat like the parent, and you may even get something better, but you could also get something that is inferior. Even from species the seed does not always come exactly true, that is one of the wonderful provisions of nature for evolving better strains; those that are better suited to their environment tend to survive and thus variations occur.

I like to sow the seed in the autumn immediately it is ripe. Lily seed is

Fig. 3. Seeds spaced in the pot and ready to be covered with a thin layer of sifted soil

thin and papery, but large enough to be handled individually. I sow it in a box or pot, that is four inches deep or so, in a mixture of soil and peat and sand (John Innes seed compost is also suitable), with holes in the bottom of the box and a $\frac{1}{2}$-inch layer of crocks or gravel for drainage. I leave the pots or boxes outside where they are exposed to all possible cold and frost during the winter. A cold frame is the best place because it can be easily closed in the event of heavy rain or snow (which makes such a mess of the soil when it thaws). But a frame is not essential, and the boxes can be left in the open so long as they are covered during heavy rain or snow. If the pots or boxes become water-logged the seeds or bulbs are liable to start to rot. The boxes should not be allowed to dry out, but be kept damp, without being sodden.

With lilies there are two types of germination; one is "epigeal" when the long cotyledon pushes upwards often lifting the seed with it, and the other is "hypogeal" germination when a tiny bulb is formed below ground before anything appears above the surface. Ideally those seeds which are hypogeal (notably *auratum*, *speciosum*, *monadelphum* and *martagon*) should be kept for about six weeks in a temperature of about 20°C. before they are put in the cold. (The amateur will appreciate that there are many methods of hastening these treatments by means of a refrigerator, a hot airing cupboard or a greenhouse). But even if it is slower, the straightforward treatment of exposure to cold in a frame throughout the winter is the simplest and very effective way for the amateur of starting the seeds; and by about March or April a green leaf will become visible.

By mid-summer the seedlings will have produced a second leaf, and then they can be pricked out in boxes at about two inches apart. John Innes potting compost No. 1 is a suitable compost. Sometimes I put them straight out in the open ground into their permanent site (each marked with a stick); but some are lost this way, especially if it turns out to be a year of extremes of weather, for they may die of drought or waterlogging. In boxes one has more control over soil conditions. The boxes can be kept in a frame in semi-shade protected only from snow and heavy rain.

Scales. Lily bulbs are made up of scales in concentric rings, each scale being attached to the base of the bulb. When these scales are detached each can be made to produce new bulbs. Healthy scales may be pulled off with the thumb and finger (it is most important that the bulb is healthy); if the bulb is in the ground, note that it is unnecessary to dig it up; dig down to it and break off as many outer scales as are required. In moderation it does the bulb no harm at all. You may like to try to induce a scale to produce more than one bulb by cutting a nick in each shoulder of the scale with a sharp knife.

Fill a box or pot, depth 5 or 6 inches, with an inch of crocks and a layer of sphagnum moss or dead leaves, and put on top of this a potting soil

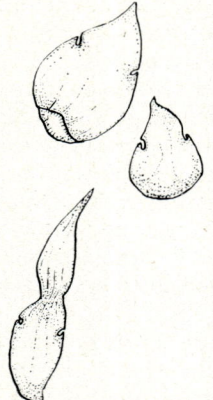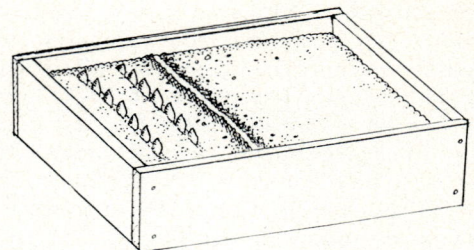

*Fig. 4. Notched scales, left; scales
inserted in the box of compost, right*

consisting of top soil, a little leaf-mould and a liberal quantity of sand almost to the top of the box, pressing it down quite firmly. With the finger make a row across the end of the box, about $\frac{1}{4}$-inch from one end, and fill it with sand. The depth of the rows will depend on the height of the particular scales, but when they are pressed down firmly and surrounded by sand, about one third of the scale should be above the surface. Then make other rows about $\frac{3}{4}$-inch apart until the box is full. Water it and put it under the staging in the potting shed, cold house or other frost-free place for the winter, just keeping the soil moist. I like to cover the box with a sheet of asbestos since this seems to keep the temperature even and preserves moisture. In the spring green leaves will begin to appear, and then the box must be brought into the light. After they have grown their second leaf, the little bulbs can be put into boxes or even into the open ground.

Some people prefer to grow their scales in a polythene bag or a jar which contains a mixture of damp sand and sphagnum moss or vermiculite plus a fungicide (quintozene, PNCB), placed in a hot cupboard or on a warm pipe. The bag or jar is kept closed in the heat to keep a uniform air humidity. It is quite easy to produce bulblets in this way, but the young bulbs have to be transferred to a box earlier than those raised in boxes; growth at this stage is more precarious and losses may be relatively high.

Scales are the easiest way of reproducing most lilies when an exact replica of the original bulb is required; the scale is part of the tissue of original bulb and must be exactly like its parent. Therefore it has that advantage over raising lilies from seed. But if the original bulb is infected by any disease, the new lilies from its scales will of course be infected too. So before using scales for propagation you must be sure that your bulbs are healthy.

Fig. 5. Propagation by scales. A. *Breaking off the scales from a bulb.*
B. *Inserting individual scales in the pot.* C. *Young plants grown from the scales.* D. *Young plants about to be transplanted*

13

Fig. 6. Propagation by bulbils

A. *The bulbils being removed from the parent stem*

B. *Then put into a pot*

C. *Young plants in the following year*

Bulblets can often be found at about ground level round the stem of a bulb. These can be detached and planted out. If they are very small it may be as well to box or pot them for a season. *Bulbils* are found (looking like black peas) up the stem at the leaf axils. These can be detached when ready to fall off and planted in rows in boxes, just below the soil level (they are most commonly found in *tigrinum* type of lily). Both of these methods of propagation are easy, but, as with scale propagation, any virus disease which the parent plant has will be carried over in the child.

14

6. The best species to grow

The choice is very difficult, but I have selected only those which are personal favourites of mine and which are also universally agreed to be easy to cultivate.

First and foremost is *Lilium regale* (the Regal lily). If ever there was a lily for everyman this is it. Flowering in July, it has a white trumpet with a golden throat and with pink markings outside, and it smells deliciously. It is easy to raise from seed, flowering within 2 or 3 years; it will tolerate any kind of soil, seems to be more resistant to disease than most and will persist for many years. The flower stem grows from 3 to 6 feet tall. These merits put it into the front rank for everyone.

Everyone will be able to grow *Lilium martagon*. It is the most widely distributed lily in the wild, extending from China through Siberia and Europe; it was thought at one time that it was native to Britain, but though it has naturalized itself in some places it is now believed to have been introduced either in Roman times or through monastic gardens in the middle ages. The pure white form is one of the most lovely of all lilies, with a green centre to the turk's cap flowers; the very dark purple forms are very beautiful too. Some of the pinks are good, but in some flowers there is a tendency for the colour to be spoiled by a bluish tint; it flowers in July. *L. martagon* will grow anywhere; I once had some surplus seed and scattered it in the fringe of the garden amongst ivy; somewhat to my surprise hundreds of lilies came up, in all shades of colour. After I had removed the ivy the large patch flourished for many years. These were grown heedlessly—if grown with care and properly cultivated in a prepared bed the spikes are magnificent. The stems will grow up to 6 feet tall. Its one disadvantage is that it comes slowly from seed—it will not flower till about the fourth year after sowing.

L. monadelphum (and its close relation *szovitsianum*) is a great lily too, and in some parts of the country has naturalized itself in a limited way. The pendulous flowers vary in colour from a brilliant butter yellow to primrose; some are heavily spotted with purple dots. It grows about 4 or 5 feet in height, and has the advantage that it blooms earlier than most lilies. On a warm evening at the end of June its scent pervades the garden, though indoors it is rather too powerful. It tolerates lime happily, and prefers half shade.

L. pardalinum (the Leopard lily) is also very easy to cultivate. In nature it is found on hummocks in swamps, but though it does not like to become dried out completely, it will stand almost any conditions of soil and position. It will grow 6 to 8 feet in height and bears a cluster of outward-facing turk's cap flowers which are orange-red in colour and spotted with brown; the usual forms are almost scentless. It flowers in July.

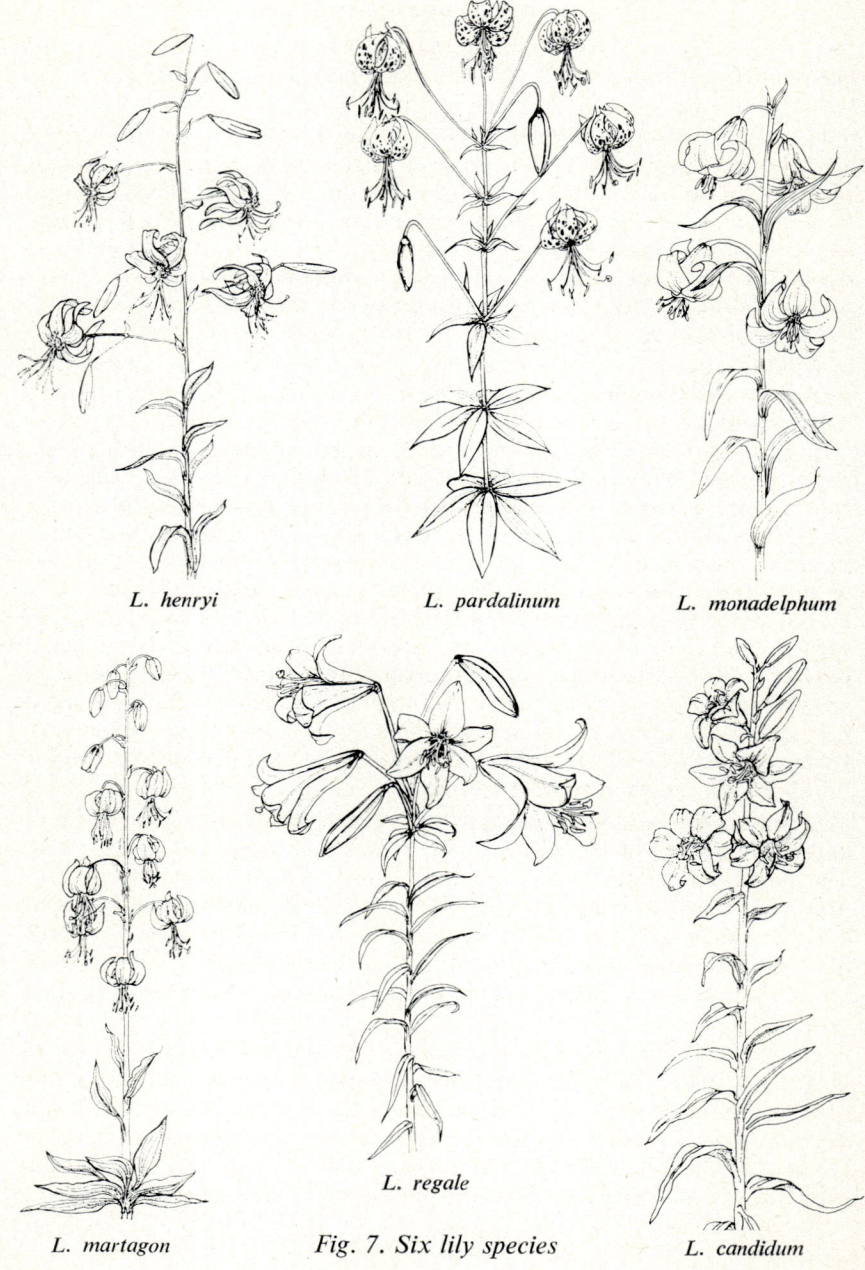

L. henryi   *L. pardalinum*   *L. monadelphum*

L. martagon   *L. regale*   *L. candidum*

Fig. 7. Six lily species

L. henryi usually grows up to 7 or 8 feet in height and is best planted behind a shrub of that height or a tall herbaceous plant such as golden rod (*Solidago*); this happens to be a good combination since golden rod flowers at the same time (August), the orange flowers of the lily showing up well against the yellow of the *Solidago*. This is one of the few lilies which really seems to prefer lime to any other soil. Flowering in August, it is a welcome late-comer.

L. candidum (the Madonna lily) I include with some hesitation. Many expert lily growers cannot grow it! But if you live in East Anglia as I do, you see masses of it growing luxuriantly in many a cottage garden in July where it is a real joy to behold, often growing in heavy clay.

Apart from its beauty it has claims on us for being the lily which has been grown for 3,000 years in gardens; the Cretans and Egyptians revered it as a medicinal plant, and it has been the emblem of the Virgin Mary during the Christian era. But it is distressingly subject to botrytis. If you wish to grow it the best plan is to beg or buy one bulb from a cottage garden, and grow a stock of it from scales of that bulb, and the probability is that your stock will be free from disease. It should be planted in September since it starts growth and produces leaves before the winter. It very seldom sets seed.

Perhaps I should include here *L.* × *testaceum*. At one time it was believed to be a species, but it is certainly a hybrid between *L. candidum* and *L. chalcedonicum*, and a very old hybrid at that. It hangs its whorl of flowers and they are of a pale saffron in colour. Like its *candidum* parent, it needs to be planted early and near the surface; it too is liable to botrytis. But it is a very beautiful lily when it thrives.

Cardiocrinum giganteum, sometimes known as *Lilium giganteum*, is one of four species of this special group. It is a woodland plant, growing up to 12 feet in height with as many as 20 flowers to a stem; these are thrust outwards and downwards from the stem and are white and shaped like a funnel, with a streak of red within. At the base is a rosette of luscious green heart-shaped leaves. When in flower the surrounding area is redolent with its wonderful scent. It flowers only once (and that after up to 10 years growth from seed!) but in the autumn half-matured bulbs cluster round the base of the stem and these can be split up and replanted, and will flower in a year or two.

Lilium auratum platyphyllum, the golden-rayed lily of Japan. This grows 4 to 7 feet in height, and its enormous white flowers, spotted with pink and streaked with gold, may be 12 inches across. It flowers in August. This is a lily which dislikes lime. It is best planted in semi-shade and amongst ferns and greenery, since it dwarfs other flowers growing near it. It is rather susceptible to virus infection.

Other much loved lilies are *parryi, duchartrei, formosanum pricei, cana-*

dense, *chalcedonicum* and *kelloggii*, but not everyone has found them easy, so that it would be dishonest to include them in the list.

7. Suggested hybrid lilies

This is a most difficult matter, and the best advice I can give is to suggest that you should look through a catalogue (and most of them are illustrated in colour), take your choice and try them. If I were driven to make a list, this would be it:

CHALICE SHAPED AND FACING UPWARDS*
Croesus. Golden yellow; June. 3 to 4 ft.
Destiny. Lemon yellow; June. 3 to 4 ft.
Enchantment. Vivid nasturtium-red (the colour kills any other near); June. 2 to 3 ft.
Harmony. Brilliant orange; June. 2 to 3 ft.
Joan Evans. Golden yellow; July. 2 to 4 ft.
Ruby (Byam's Ruby). Blood red; June-July. 2 ft.

OUTWARD FACING
Paprika. Blood crimson; June. 2 to 3 ft.
Prosperity. Lemon yellow; June. 3 to 4 ft.
Redbird. Medium orange-red; July. 4 to 5 ft.

PENDENT
Amber Gold. Buttercup yellow; June-July. 4 to 5 ft.
Burgundy Strain. Shades of cherry red, burgundy and claret; July. 3 to 5 ft.
Citronella. Golden to lemon yellow; July. 3 to 4 ft.
Edith Cecilia. Creamy pink shading to rose pink, spotted; July. 2 to 3 ft.
Fiesta Hybrids. Colour range from yellow to orange-red; July. 3 to 5 ft.
Fuga. Bright orange, spotted; June-July. 3 to 4 ft.
Joseph Fletcher. Very dark crimson; June-July. 3 to 4 ft.
Maxwill. Bright orange-red; July-August. 4 to 5 ft.
Pink Charm. Pink with creamy centre; June-July. 2 to 3 ft.
Sonata. Pale orange to pink; July. 4 to 5 ft.
Sutter's Gold. Deep yellow, turk's cap; July. 3 to 4 ft.

MARTAGON HYBRIDS
Marhan. Orange with reddish spots; June-July. 4 to 5 ft.
Mrs. R. O. Backhouse. Orange-yellow spotted purple; June-July. 4 to 5 ft.
Paisley Strain. From white through yellow, orange, mahogany to lilac, with small maroon spots; June. 3 to 5 ft.

*The grouping of hybrid lilies is based on parentage, and flower shape and carriage.

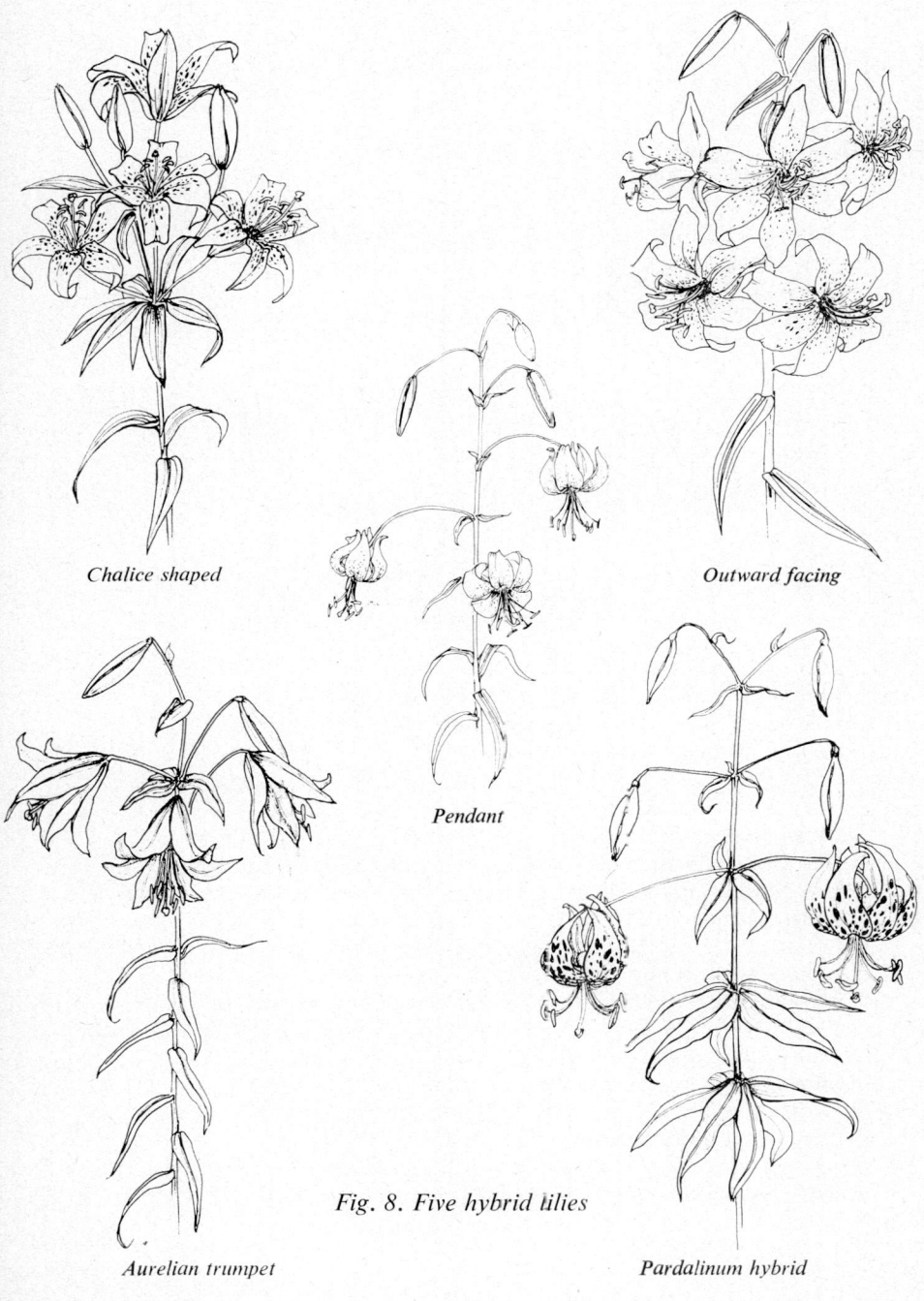

Chalice shaped

Outward facing

Pendant

Aurelian trumpet

Fig. 8. Five hybrid lilies

Pardalinum hybrid

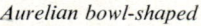
Aurelian bowl-shaped   *Oriental hybrid*

Fig. 9. Left: a bowl-shaped aurelian; right: an oriental hybrid

PARDALINUM HYBRIDS
Afterglow. Crimson red with yellow centres; June. 6 ft.
Buttercup. Bright yellow, scented; June-July. 4 to 5 ft.
Shuksan. Yellowish orange; July. 4 to 5 ft.

AURELIAN (trumpet types)
African Queen. Rich yellow; July. 5 to 6 ft.
Black Dragon. White with dark red reverse; late July. 5 to 8 ft.
Black Magic. Similar to Black Dragon, but flowering in July-August.
Golden Splendor. Deep yellow with maroon stripe on the reverse; July. 3 to 6 ft.
Green Dragon. White with chartreuse green reverse; July. 3 to 6 ft.
Limelight. Lime yellow with greenish tinge on outside of petals; July. 3 to 5 ft.
Royal Gold. Golden yellow; July. 3 to 5 ft.
Sentinel. White with golden throat; June-July. 3 to 5 ft.

AURELIAN (bowl-shaped)
Bright Star. Ivory white outside, apricot-orange inside; mid-July. 4 ft.
Golden Sunburst. Bright yellow; July-August. 4 to 6 ft.

Pink Sunburst Strain. White or green suffused fuchsia-pink; July-August, 4 to 5 ft.
Stardust. White with orange centre star; July-August. 4 to 5 ft.
Thunderbolt. Tangerine orange; July-August. 6 ft.

ORIENTALS (speciosum and auratum hybrids)
American Eagle. White spotted light vermilion; August. 4 to 5 ft.
Black Beauty. Very dark red; August. 5 to 6 ft.
Empress of India. Warm crimson red with darker central vein; August. 4 to 5 ft.
Imperial Crimson. Shades of deep crimson red with white margins; August. 5 to 7 ft.
Imperial Gold. Ivory white with central yellow band to each petal; August. 4 to 6 ft.
Imperial Silver. White spotted vermilion; August. 5 to 6 ft.
Jamboree. Crimson red with narrow white margins; August. 5 to 6 ft.
Journey's End. Bengal rose with a narrow white margin; August. 4 to 5 ft.
Magic Pink. Pink, large; June. 3 ft.
Pink Glory Strain. Salmon-pink, generally with a narrow white margin; July-August. 5 to 6 ft.
Red Band Hybrids. Bright crimson red to rich vermilion with white borders; August. 4 to 5 ft.
Snowflake. White with soft lavender pink flecks; August. 4 to 5 ft.

8. Pests and diseases

Rabbits will gladly devour the leaves and stem of a lily; grey squirrels and field mice enjoy a luscious bulb, even if a crocus is a still more delectable meal. It is not easy to prevent damage caused by small mammals. Traps may sometimes be used, but a local reduction in numbers by trapping is usually soon made good by more individuals moving in from surrounding areas. Various mechanical repellents such as gorse stems or sharp-edged stones, or chemical repellents, such as foul smelling rabbit smears, may work for a time but the only sure way of protecting valuable stocks of lilies is to use netting around clumps of plants or around the garden.

Leather-jackets, wireworms and millipedes are all partial to bulbs; out slugs are the greatest enemy. I once grew a very rare lily and it had ten buds on it; one night a slug climbed the stem and ate through it below the top eight buds. Never anywhere, as far as I know, has it (a white *polyphyllum*) been grown as well again and I have never forgiven that loathsome slug. Unceasing warfare must be waged against them, and so far as the bulbs are concerned a good deal of course sand round the bulb and at the base of the stem is a considerable deterrent. Slug baits based on methiocarb (Draza) or metaldehyde may be used to reduce slug populations and the removal and destruction of any unnecessary accumulations of plant debris will help to limit them.

The other main enemy is the aphis, since it is through their agency that virus diseases are carried. An aphis sucks the juice from a lily stem or leaf, and if that lily has a virus infection the aphis will infect the next lily which it visits—just as a mosquito conveys malaria from one human being to another. Some lilies (notably *L. tigrinum*) can be infected by one type of virus without showing it, but in most the leaves soon become mottled or show yellow streaks and they may become distorted. The buds may also be contorted and fail to open properly. Severely affected plants are stunted and may die down early. Virus-infected plants cannot be cured and should be burned. It is therefore important to keep all aphids in check in any garden where lilies are grown.

Modern systemic insecticides based on dimethoate or formothion are very effective and may be applied as sprays at something like monthly intervals during the spring and early summer, when aphids tend to be most active. Non-systemic insecticides such as malathion or BHC may also be used but are unlikely to be so effective or persistent.

The "lily disease" or leaf blight caused by the fungus *Botrytis elliptica* will affect any lily. It is often associated with a wet season. In their native habitat most lilies do not often become wet at the time they are in full leaf and flower, but in this country the flowering season in July is often very wet, so that this is an affliction especially troublesome in Britain. The first indications on the leaves are dark green water-soaked oval-shaped spots which soon turn brown and then white. In severe attacks the leaves wither from the base of the stem upwards, and the flower buds are injured so that they produce distorted flowers, or they may be killed. Sometimes the fungus enters the main flowering stem causing it to fall over and rot. Since the fungus spores are air-borne, it is important to pick off and burn infected leaves and stems. It can survive the winter, and the leaves of any infected plant should be collected and burned in the autumn. This disease can be controlled by spraying at about fortnightly intervals with a copper fungicide such as bordeaux mixture, starting as soon as the flower buds can be seen. There is normally no need to destroy the bulbs of plants affected by this disease as in most cases they remain healthy, but if they should show signs of rotting they should be burned.

Another unpleasant disease is basal rot, and it probably kills more lilies than does any other plague. The roots wither away and there appears on the base of the bulb a spongy brown mass; gradually the bulb falls apart. This trouble can occur as a result of too wet soil conditions, but similar symptoms can be caused by several different fungi which can only be identified by means of a microscope. Affected bulbs should, therefore, be sent to an expert so that the exact cause of the trouble can be determined and appropriate control measures can then be recommended.

It has recently been found that the fungicide benomyl is very effective for the control of botrytis and basal rot, but it is not available for use on lilies in this country yet.

It should be mentioned that lilies can be attacked by eel worm and this can kill them. So many as 900 have been found in one bulb, Theoretically they can be killed by immersion in hot water under controlled conditions, but this cannot usually be undertaken by an amateur. Removing and burning infected plants will help limit the spread of these pests. The symptoms of certain diseases and other disorders are easily confused with eelworm symptoms and such drastic measures should only be taken after specialist examination has confirmed that eelworm is present.

The R.H.S. Lily Group

This group is for Fellows of the Royal Horticultural Society, with a special interest in lilies. No extra subscription is required.

The group was started in 1931; meetings and excursions to gardens are arranged during the lily season, and a seed exchange between members is organised annually.

In addition a great deal of information on lilies and their cultivation is available in the Lily Year Books published since 1932 by the Royal Horticultural Society. Copies of many of these are still available.

For information on the Lily Group and the Lily Year Books write to the Secretary, The Royal Horticultural Society, P.O. Box 313, Vincent Square, London SW1P 2PE.

Printed in England by
Harrison and Sons Ltd., Hayes, Middx.